Love Being the Boss Hate Business

Simple Steps to Building a Solid Business Foundation for your Enterprise. So you can focus on what makes you money.

Susan Lane • Ali Bagley

Love Being the Boss, Hate Business

Copyright © 2021 Ali Bagley and Susan Lane

All rights reserved.

ISBN: 9798413513705

Love Being the Boss, Hate Business

Thank you to everyone who made our journey difficult, we learned the most from you
Thank you to everybody who believed in us, we were able to grow with your support
Thank you to everyone who gave us an opportunity to learn and develop our skills

But most of all thank you to those who we love and love us back, you have made the journey worthwhile

Love Being the Boss, Hate Business

LANE
BAGLEY

CONTENTS

	Foreword By Marco Bertagni, CEO	Pg 6
	Introduction	Pg 8
Step 1	Assess your Entrepreneurship (you da boss!)	Pg 11
Step 2	Nailing your Niche (target practice)	Pg 21
Step 3	Visibility in your marketplace (get seen)	Pg 35
Step 4	Do the Math (show me the money)	Pg 45
Step 5	Plan for Success (you gotta have one)	Pg 55
Step 6	Business Operations (the icky admin stuff)	Pg 63
Step 7	Equipment and Software (stuff you gotta get)	Pg 71
Step 8	The Business of Business (clients and stuff)	Pg 79
Step 9	Website (where the interaction happens)	Pg 91
Step 10	Marketing & Distribution (get out there)	Pg 107
Step 11	LAUNCH YOUR BUSINESS	Pg 119
	Next Steps: Planning For Growth	Pg 121
	Final Words: Tips for Success	Pg 127
BONUS SECTIONS	Extra Notes Pages for You	Pg 132
	About The Authors	Pg 152
	Recommended Further Reading	Pg 154
	Business We Recommend	Pg 155

Love Being the Boss, Hate Business

FOREWORD
By Marco Bertagni, CEO of Bertagni Consulting

I love being the Boos, but I really do not enjoy all of the extra stuff that I have to do just to keep everything running smoothly day to day.

I've been running my international consulting firm for over 12 years and now I have help to do the day-to-day stuff, but when I started out, not only was I unaware of all the stuff that needed doing but I had no money to pay anyone to tell me or do it for me.

I wish I had been able to get this book back then. It would have saved me hours of work and a lot of money.

I like to:

- Travel and meet people
- Support my clients in growing their businesses
- Do public speaking engagements
- Experience different cultures
- Take a break in the day to play cards with my friend

Nothing on this list relates even remotely to marketing, admin, accounting, social media or budgeting. I know they need to be done, but they suck up my card playing time and that's not good for me.

What I love about this book it that it shows you, in simple terms what needs to be done, how to go about it and where to find the information you need. It's like a map for success, and anyone who knows me knows that maps are my passion.

The additional notes pages and action plans are brilliant and it's so handy having them in the book instead of random sheets of paper that I will never find again!

Ali and Susan have spent years in business, they know what they are talking about, in fact Ali provides business services into my company because I know that my business is safe in her hands.

Read, absorb, learn and action, this book is what your business has been crying out for.

Marco

Love Being the Boss, Hate Business

INTRODUCTION
Why you need THIS book

When we started our businesses, we had absolutely no idea of the work that would be involved in just running the business, never mind what we actually delivered to our clients. There was so much stuff we discovered that we had to deal with, and frankly it was pretty overwhelming.

From the basic administration through to the equipment we needed and all the legal and logistical considerations we had to navigate. So many things to think about and do, to just get started, never mind get visible.

When we met and started to talk about our businesses, we realised that we had both had similar experiences setting up and running them in our first few months.

We had both considered giving up, and not because we were not absolutely sure of our abilities in delivering our services and adding value to our clients by solving their problems with those services. It was because the rest of the administrative businessy stuff was so stressful and time consuming and we had made expensive mistakes.

We both come from business development and project management backgrounds in corporate, we know about business management on a corporate scale, and we understand the need for a solid foundation for our businesses. We were not however prepared for the work we needed to do, to adapt what we already knew, for a small independent business.

Being a Boss and running a successful business is so much more than just getting your service or product ready to go and getting started.

What we really could have done with, to save us time and money and relieve the stress, was a guide to take us through the steps we needed to follow.

Months of research and testing later we bring you that guide, for YOUR business. Step by step everything you need to consider, to build a solid foundation for your business.

Our businesses are successful not only because we are great at what we do. They are successful because they have been built on a solid foundation that frees us up to do what we love best . . . helping you.

So, thank you for investing in yourself and your business by purchasing this book.

Thank you for taking the time to read it and learn from it.

We wish you every success in your business,

Ali & Susan

Love Being the Boss, Hate Business

: Love Being the Boss, Hate Business

STEP 1
ASSESS YOUR ENTREPRENEURSHIP
(you da boss!)

"If you're starting something on your own, you better have a passion for it, because this is hard work."

Sallie Krawcheck, Co-founder of Ellevest

Are you cut out to be an entrepreneur?

The path of an entrepreneur isn't any easy one. Many have tried and failed. Though it is a path of risk and uncertainty, it also brings incredible opportunity, freedom and achievement.

On the surface, entrepreneurship appears exciting and liberating. However, like an iceberg, there's so much more just below the surface, if you only look a little deeper. As an entrepreneur, the success of your business rests entirely in your hands.

If you value security and certainty above all else, then entrepreneurship is likely not for you. Therefore, it is important as you start out on your journey to set up your business, that you consider both the opportunities and the risks.

Key considerations:

Reset your mindset

Entrepreneurs have a robust worth ethic. They are ambitious, creative, confident, disciplined, persistent and extremely resourceful. It is important to ask yourself, 'do I have these characteristics?'

Consider your mindset. Are you optimistic? Are you willing and able to learn and adapt?

Don't just focus on the positive outcomes. Take time and consider, if this doesn't go to plan, what impact will that have? Will a slow start deplete your self-belief, enthusiasm and drive? Do you view failure as a stop sign, as feedback, or a learning experience on what to refine in order to move forward? Do you truly believe in what you have to offer and how that will benefit people?

Be honest with yourself. Realistic. Assess your fears and potential obstacles and make a plan for how you will manage them. They may not all materialize, but some of them will. In these situations, how you react will determine your success.

Mindset is everything. Our brains are designed to believe everything we tell it.

What you believe is what you can achieve

Motivation

Successful entrepreneurs have a compelling vision that motivates and moves them forward every day. They deliver on their vision by setting BIG goals. They use daily process goals to take action, stay focused and motivated, and milestone or progress goals to measure their achievement.

Do you have a compelling vision and reason for your business? On a scale of 1 – 10 decide how motivated are you? Your degree of motivation will drive your degree of commitment. You need to honestly assess your desire, motivation, fears, obstacles, and options for starting your business.

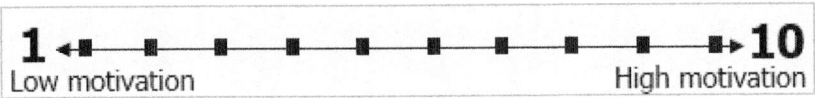

Commitment

Entrepreneurs go all in on their well-researched and developed ideas. Note the phrase *'well-researched and developed'* because you will never succeed on an idea alone. Self-starters are fully committed, every day, to take the necessary action to move them forward to deliver on their vision. Their success is dependent on their motivation and drive.

However, there is always a price to pay for success. Do you have the resources and tenacity to stay the course? Rome wasn't built in a day, and neither is a sustainable, profitable business. It takes time to build your brand and build a community. Do you get discouraged easily? Are you prepared to put in whatever hours are necessary to build your business? Could working long hours to achieve your vision put strain or stress on other areas of your life? Or in your personal relationships? Do you have a network who are committed to support you as you build your business? Do you have what it takes to go the distance?

Purposeful, intentful, commitment. Working every day, in an organised and planned manner, will determine your ability to deliver on your dreams.

So many business owners we know jumped straight in and thought clients and sales would just flow in and their business would take off. It's not like that though, is it? Growth, foundation and resilience are necessary. It has taken us time to grow our businesses into the thriving operations they are today. It will take you time as well.

Finances and administration

To succeed, you will need some knowledge and understanding of how to run and operate a business. Building any business from the ground up takes time.

It is important to align your business expectations from the outset. Is this a full-time, part-time or side-hustle business for you? Do you have the funds to start-up, or do you need to raise capital? How soon does the business need to be able to provide a sustainable income? Have you set a budget that matches this timeframe?

Do you have the time to build a business? Do you understand that running a business is more than just providing services or selling products ? It needs time set aside to manage the business operations and continually develop content.

Do you understand what is required to start a business in terms of registration, registering patents and trademarks, legal contracts, setting up bank accounts, managing invoices and payments, paying expense, accounting, taxes, annual reporting obligations, purchasing and maintaining software and equipment, getting insurances set up, launching marketing campaigns and managing social media and so much more . . .

From the outset you need to commit to running a professional business in a professional manner. Create the discipline to do what you have to do, when you have to do it, so you can do what you want to do the rest of the time.

Resources

An honest assessment of your strengths and weakness is vital. No-one can do everything, certainly not well. There is a big difference between, *I do not know how to do this* versus *I do not want to do this.*

From the outset, determine what resources you need for your business, what you may need help with, and when. Take this into consideration when setting your budget and allocate funds where they are truly needed.

Consider this: you may hate doing your financial accounts, but you **can** do them; alternatively, you may need a website but have no idea **how** to build one. In this example your budget should allocate funds to hiring an expert web designer as an immediate priority however for now, you do the accounts and look to engage a bookkeeper when the business is up and running and making money.

Identifying the areas where professional help or skills are needed will help you save time and money and enable you to launch your business operations in way that sets you up for success.

Values

Now is a great time to think about your personal and company's values. Why? Knowing you values means knowing yourself and what you stand for. Knowing your values helps you to make decisions and take action to move you towards your personal and business goals.

Knowing your personal and business values will help you define your brand and will also align you with how you intend to act as a

Love Being the Boss, Hate Business

Boss and how you will run your business. Once defined you can use you values to help you define what success look likes and means to you, how you can measure it and how you can use this to grow your business.

Below is a list of our values to help you with this exercise. Or alternatively there are numerous free questionnaires and assessments you can take online.

Values that we attach to our businesses:

Integrity	Autonomy	Balance
Authenticity	Compassion	Fun
Understanding	Adventure	Acceptance
Hard work	Innovation	Calm
Honesty	Discovery	Community
Support	Boldness	Service
Caring	Creativity	Gratitude
Achievement	Growth	Trust
Empathy	Collaboration	Responsibility
Purpose	Friendship	Knowledge

Your vision for your business

What do you see when you think about what your business will become? Are you working part time and looking for a steady flow of a few clients or sales a week or are you the next Richard Branson? Whatever your vision, it is key to your success.

It is important to remember and hold onto that vision and keep moving towards it every day.

It is harder in the beginning as you battle your way through everything unfamiliar territory and it's easy to start feeling overwhelmed and defeated as all your time and energy is being consumed to just get you out of the starter gates, rather than actually doing what you love. This will change.

Stay the course. Write down your vision, do it now, right here.

Now find a picture or object that represents your vision and keep that in your workspace as a reminder on those difficult days to keep going.

Celebrate every step achieved on your journey towards realizing your vision and learn from every setback.

A few more thoughts . . .

Every business owner needs a coach (every business owner).

Find a coach that gives you support where you need it. If you are not strong on the administration, hire a business coach. If you need help staying focused, motivated and positive about the long journey to success, find a mindset coach.

If you struggle with creating content for your website and social media, hire a writers coach.

Figure out what you need and get the help to keep you accountable and moving forward.

An entrepreneur's journey is both challenging and rewarding however facing these difficulties and solving problems can provide you with an incredible opportunity to build a business and lifestyle you love.

The basic key elements to growing a successful business are:

- Having a clear vision (researched and developed!)
- Commitment to work daily and progressively to achieve your goals
- Being honest and realistic about what you can achieve v's where you will need help
- A mindset aligned with your expectations

If you have these basic elements in place, and we haven't scared you to death yet, then read on . . . The chapters in this book have all been designed to help you, the new entrepreneur, to build and maintain a solid and successful business to take you closer to your dreams.

CHECKLIST - ASSESS YOUR ENTREPRENEURSHIP

Security and certainty are not my key drivers	☐
I have a robust work ethic	☐
I have a compelling vision that motivates me	☐
I have a well researched and developed business idea	☐
I have a comprehensive and realistic budget for my business	☐
I understand that business is about more than clients and sales	☐
I will continually reassess the resources I need	☐
I will engage a coach to support me in developing my business	☐

So now you know you have what it takes, what's next?

Love Being the Boss, Hate Business

My Notes and Observations

My Notes and Observations

Love Being the Boss, Hate Business

STEP 2
NAILING YOUR NICHE
(Target Practice)

"When you find your niche, you just gotta continue to be confident and thrive in it".

D'Angelo Russell

Nailing your Niche is, in our opinion, one of the most vital steps in building a successful base for your business.

Is your key struggle finding and onboarding clients? Do you have a service (or a product) that you believe in and that you are sure people will want to buy but you aren't getting the interest you expected? Are things a lot harder than you imagined they would be?

Chances are that you are taking somewhat of a scatter gun approach, posting here there and everywhere, advertising all over social media, but with no clear idea of how to engage with the people who will actually want what you are offering.

Maybe your message is too generic so prospective clients can't really see the benefit they will get from buying from you? And seriously, when have you ever bought anything that didn't benefit you in some way right?

If all this is true, or even some of it, then we are willing to bet you haven't nailed your niche yet.

Let's get started . . .

Why can't I just try to sell to everybody?
'Jack of all trades, master of none'

As a business owner once you have developed all of the skills you need, gained all the qualifications you need, done all the training you need and invested hours and probably thousands on getting set up, you will more than likely be able to sell to anyone who comes to you who is interested in your product or your service.

The issue here is . . . and we cannot state this enough . . .

If you don't target your marketing to a niche audience, no one will know what you are about, what your offer means to them or what you can do for them.

So why would they come to you in the first place?

People buy from people they know like and trust, but even then, they will only buy what benefits them. Whatever you are selling is never, in any world we know off, going to be of benefit to everybody. In fact, your particular service or product may only benefit a tiny proportion of the world's population.

Unless you are Steve Jobs right? When he introduced the original iPhone, Steve Jobs said that Apple's goal for the first year of the iPhone was to capture 1% of the worldwide cellphone market. The company achieved that goal and now stands at somewhere around 30% of the market[1].

About 75% of the worlds' population own a cellphone, that's approximately 5.8bn people. Apple have 30% share of that, approximately 1.7 bn, which is only about 20% of the worlds' population. And I guarantee you, they have a very powerful niche!

So, what is a niche

The dictionary definition of 'Niche' that counts here is:

'A specialized segment of the market for a particular kind of product or service'.

Your niche is: *Your corner of the market, Your place, Your specialty, Your 'thing'.*

Your clearly defined niche is your specialized segment of the market for your product or service.

Are you thinking right now 'but what I offer isn't specialized, loads of people do it, how can I have a niche that is specialized'?

If so, then you have 2 choices:

---

[1] As at end 2020

1. Redesign your service or product to make it unique, special or different, or. . .

2. Define your unique, special and different way of delivering it or using it or the unique and special benefit that it offers to your prospective clients.

Why do I need a Niche for my business?

Without clarity on exactly what you do, how you do it, who you do it for and what they will get from it, you cannot streamline and target your marketing. If you cannot target your marketing than it is much harder to connect with prospective clients who want what you are offering.

This can lead to very expensive and time-consuming mistakes. A successful business plan may have some contingency for error but will never propose a strategy that includes wasting time and money, right?

Can I have several niches? we hear you ask. Well in theory yes you can. Particularly where you have multiple products to sell. Let's look at multiple niching in service provision first.

Multiple service niches

I begin this by saying that if you are a one-man/woman band operation then try not to spread yourself too thin. If you are going to market several niches, then you will spend all your time marketing and no time delivering and making money.

Stick to a max of three niches but in doing so, make sure that they all resonate with your overarching business mission statement.

By example let's say that you have three niches which specialize in coaching individuals, coaching businessowners and coaching coaches. All three speak to your overarching mission statement which is:

I help people to overcome overwhelm, build self-confidence and create awesome motivation in order to reach their full personal and professional potential.

Can you see how they fit? Just remember the more niches, the busier you are going to be targeting each one individually.

Multiple product niches

If you are selling products, it is likely that you have more than one product, possibly many. The first step is to bundle your products into complimentary ranges and aim for no more than 3 ranges. (More than that and you are either really overstretching yourself or you need staff!).

Then niche each range and market them according to their individual niche markets.

For instance: You have a business which sells products for wellbeing and relaxation. This might split into three ranges such as:

Bath time relaxation – candles, bath products, towels etc.

Outdoor recreation – protective creams, thick socks for walking, pedometers etc.

Massage products – oils, creams, towels, books etc.

There may be one person who would want all of that. More likely that your ideal client for each of these ranges is different (and we are going to generalize here because it is impossible to be specific about your products and clients in a book designed for all small business owners).

Bath time relaxation – hard working parents who want a bit of me time, like to just relax away from it all in an ocean of calm and peace. Read a book, have a glass of wine etc.

Outdoor recreation – men and women who exercise, like to be outdoors, value their health and wellbeing so they exercise and eat well etc.

Love Being the Boss, Hate Business

Massage products – people who like to be indulged, taken care of, who like a 'treat'.

Can you see now how different products speak to different markets? You run a company offering well-being and relaxation but that means different things to different clients. To reach those different clients you need to niche your product ranges.

How do I find my 'Niche'?

The 5 key steps to nailing your Niche

1. Clearly identify your ideal client
2. Identify what is special about you
   a. List the experience do you have
   b. List the qualifications do you have
   c. List where you have been recognized in a specific field
3. Identify your passion, your mission, your joy
4. Identify what you specifically offer to your Ideal client?
5. Identify the benefit your client gets from your service or product

Step 1. Identify your ideal client

The first step to creating your niche is truly, madly, deeply understanding who your ideal client is. This needs to be done in some detail, the clearer the description is the more niched you can be.

Exercise 1. Get a pen and paper and using the template provided below write out the description of your Ideal Client. Write it as story, not just a list.

For instance: My ideal client is . . .

. . . a forty-year-old woman who is a new business owner wanting to grow her pet supplies business online since the pandemic has stunted her high street business.

She balances her business with caring for her husband and two teenage children, she does the lion's share of the domestic stuff and is a taxi service for her kids to get to their clubs and other interests.

As much detail as you can, make this person real in your mind.

My Ideal Client is . . .

Write your ideal client's story here:

Step 2. What is special about you?

This is about your uniqueness. If you are providing a service, it is very much about you as a person. If you are selling a product, range of products this is more about your company.

For service providers this is about your life experience, what you have gone through, what you have overcome, what resonates with you, what you have achieved, why you want to help people and what you have in common with your ideal client.

For companies selling products this is about your business ethics and values, your business story, how you started, what has been achieved, why you are the best and what your mission is.

Exercise 2. Write the story of you (your business), in detail. When you have done it get someone else to read it back to you and see how that makes you feel. Would you buy from you?

When you know how special you are, you will gain an insight into how you can really resonate with, and so benefit your ideal client.

The story of my business:

Step 3. Your Passion, Your Mission, Your Joy

This might seem a strange thing to consider when thinking about your niche. 'Isn't niching about the client' we hear you ask. Well, we are glad you asked that question.

In order to resonate with your client, you have to be passionate about what you provide, be it a service or a product. If you are not passionate about it, if it doesn't bring you joy, if you don't believe in it, then how can you possibly expect others to buy into it?

Exercise 3. Answer these questions (not in your head, write them down using the template below:

1. *What do you love and why?*

2. *Who are you really excited to work with?*

3. *What challenges do you most like to find solutions to?*

4. *What difference do you want to make in the world?*

Once you have done that consider this. If you could summarize all that into one statement, what would it say? Here is an example;

I love working with new business owners to help them identify their key skills and mission, find their niche and develop their offering to their clients.

I get so excited seeing the lightbulb moments when they realize that it's not nearly as complicated as they thought it would be and that they do have the power within them to attract the clients they really want.

Through my service I save my clients time and money, giving them opportunities, they might not otherwise have been able to pursue.

Step 4. What is it that I sell to my Ideal client?

This final step is really, really unique to you and your business.

It will vary according to whether it is a service or a product you are providing.

It will vary between corporate clients and individuals.

Exercise 4. Write down exactly what your service or product is. A clear description of exactly what you do or what you sell. And most importantly, how is it different to what everybody else is doing or selling. Really think about the problem you are solving with your product or services.

Once you have that, your ideal client description, your reasons why you are special and your mission statement, onwards and upwards, you are ready for the final step.

> My Business sells:
>
> And is unique because:

Step 5. What benefit is your client going to get from your product or service?

This is crucial, seriously. You can have the most amazing service or product, at the best price, but if it does not provide your ideal client with at least one benefit then they are not going to buy it. This is not about what your client thinks they want; this is about what they really want.

It is the final piece of information you need to nail down your niche so. . .

Exercise 5. Identify how your service or product is going to benefit your ideal client. Not just any client, just the ideal client you described earlier.

1. What will they get if they use your service or buy your product?

2. How will their life be better?

3. How will it change how they feel about themselves?

4. How will it help them to live a better, more productive life?

Once you have this and all of the results from your previous exercises you will be ready to nail down your niche.

Next Step - The Niche Formula

How do you nail down your niche from all the information you have just developed?

Here is the simple formula for nailing your niche . . .

Using all of the information you now have about your ideal client, what is special about you, your joy statement and the specifics of your service or product complete the following sentence:

'**I help** [*summary of my ideal client*] **to overcome** [*ideal clients pain point, challenge, what keeps them awake at night*] **through** [*special elements of your service or product*] **to** [*benefit your* *client receives from your service or product]*'.

This is your niche

For example

I help new and struggling business owners **to overcome** the challenge of attracting core clients and find their niche market, **through** a bespoke support coaching program designed specifically for them, **to** make the complicated simple, kick out the unnecessary and supercharge their business.

So, you have what it takes,

and you know who you serve, why and how.

What's next?

Love Being the Boss, Hate Business

My Notes and Observations

Love Being the Boss, Hate Business

My Notes and Observations

Love Being the Boss, Hate Business

STEP 3
YOUR VISIBILITY IN THE MARKETPLACE
(get seen)

"It's important to realize that brand is much more than a logo and slogan. A brand is who your company is: how you function and make decisions."

Joanna McFarland, Co-founder of HopSkipDrive

Your brand

As a business owner, **you are your organisations most valuable asset**. You are your brand. You are truly irreplaceable. Even if you provide a service or product that is already out there you do things differently. With a defined niche and clear message there is absolutely room for you to make an impact within your target market if you make yourself visible.

In any business it is vital that you stand out from the crowd. If you are the most valuable asset of your business, then consider your brand as the personality of the business. Your brand is your identity, how you present yourself to the world and what you want to be known for. How will people talk about you when you are not in the room? Your brand encompasses the emotion, imagery and associations your clients and customers will connect with in your business. This means your logo, colour scheme, and strapline need to be designed and used in clear and consistent manner. And for goodness' sake make sure your contact details and bio are everywhere you might get seen.

Your brand is so much more than colour schemes and logos. It is the essence of who you are and what you do. It is helpful to analyse how you plan to help your clients in distinct pillars. These pillars will then be the foundation for your brand and will communicate your message to the world.

Illustrated below (**Fig 3.1**) is a brand and messaging example for a Fitness Coach. In this example clients and potential clients can expect their Fitness Coach to be repeatedly and consistently discussing and offering products and services that fall under their brand pillars. Staying on brand is the key to successfully and consistently demonstrating how you can help your clients and growing your business.

	BRAND PILLARS			
	Exercise	**Health**	**Mindset**	**Fun**
Messaging	Cardio workouts	Food journal	Setting priorities	Team events
	Strength training	Food knowledge	Bad habits	Accountability buddies
	Workout programs	Recipes	Routine & discipline	Local group classes
	Yoga	Obesity & disease	Limiting beliefs	Family weekend exercise ideas
	HITT	Calculating macros / calories	Managing your time	Outdoor classes

Fig 3.1: Brand Pillars

What are your brand Pillars?

	BRAND PILLARS			
Messaging				

In most businesses you are creating a brand around your expertise, which will portray you as a leader in your field. Your brand should clearly articulate your niche, what you do and how you will help your clients. Consider brand association carefully too. How will your audience identify and relate to you?

For instance, maybe you are a Career Coach who works specifically with people who have lost their jobs; make sure that your messaging is not solely built around redundancy as a keyword. Otherwise, you could easily become known as the redundant coach! Not quite what you hoped for, right?

Finally, while your brand is all about you, your messaging is always about your clients.

1. What are their pain points?
2. What help do they need?
3. What problem are you solving?

Market research

Market research is the next step. You must develop a good understanding of your competitors and what they are doing in your field of expertise:

- How are they are positioning themselves to help their client?
- What are other businesses in your niche offering?
- How are others being clear on their brand?
- How do you plan to do it differently? better?
- What gap in the marketplace do you intend to fill?

Consider your mentors too, who is a voice of influence for you? How and why do they resonate with you? Become familiar with your competitors and identify and capitalise on where you feel they are falling short.

SWOT analysis

In order to analyse your competitors, use a SWOT analysis. This will help you to determine their Strengths, Weaknesses, Opportunities and Threats and so help you to learn about what works, what doesn't and what you can offer that is better or different (or both). ***Fig 3.2*** below is a typical SWOT grid.

	STRENGTHS	WEAKNESSES	
Things I can use for my business			Things I can learn from and avoid
	OPPORTUNITIES	THREATS	

Fig 3.2: SWOT Grid

Talk to your audience

Test the market. This will help you refine your offer. A quick and relatively easy way to do is to start a pop-up Facebook Group and share ideas around what you are offering to gain feedback on how this is perceived, or what your audience is really looking for.

Talk and connect with your audience. Remember this is not a sales pitch! Make sure this is a free group to attend and provide good quality content and you will get a wider participation and start to grow your community.

Another key consideration is the name of your business.

As much as possible you want to pick a domain name that does what it says on the label. In other words, it articulates your brand. Google loves this and it is a huge boost to your SEO (Search Engine Optimization) success.

The majority of service providers name and brand their business on themselves however, unless you are already globally well known, then this probably won't help you much in getting visibility with google.

You need to work closely with your website designer on SEO optimisation and use of keywords in your metadata to boost your visibility. Completing your free business profile on Google My Business is also a step to becoming visible online and promoting your brand.

Be prepared, building a brand does not happen overnight. It takes work, time and consistency in presence and messaging to create, build and grow. You can also expect your brand to expand over time as your clients and their needs develop.

All successful entrepreneurs will tell you that they connect and work with mentors they admire. Build your community, not just with clients but with other talented business owners in your field who understand your business market and how it works. Having a network to share ideas and experience is a great way to receive honest and reliable feedback, learn new tools and techniques and broaden your perspectives. Competition is healthy, remember, a rising tide floats all boats!

Love Being the Boss, Hate Business

CHECKLIST - **YOUR VISIBILITY IN THE MARKETPLACE**

- [ ] I have a brand that demonstrates who I am / what I sell
- [ ] I have done my market research
- [ ] I have analysed the competition and learned from them
- [ ] I have tested my marketplace
- [ ] I am focused on building my business community
- [ ] I have a strategy for being seen in my marketplace

So, you have what it takes,

and you know who you serve, why and how,

and you know there's a market for your business and what you want to look like.

So, What's next?

My Notes and Observations

My Notes and Observations

Love Being the Boss, Hate Business

My Notes and Observations

Love Being the Boss, Hate Business

STEP 4
DO THE MATH
(show me the money)

"You know you are on the road to success if you would do your job, and not be paid for it."

Oprah Winfrey

Introduction

Money, it's why we are in business right? Yes, you love what you do, yes, you'd do it for nothing if you didn't need the money, but you do, don't you? And there is more to money in business than just making it, and also between making it and taking it home. This step will look at money in your business, getting it, managing it, and keeping it.

Draft your budget

Probably the most important step after niching is developing your budget for your business.

How much do you want to make a year? – well you need to budget for that.

How much will you have to spend a year? – well you need to budget for that too.

What if things go wrong? – yes you guessed it, budget for that too.

And of course, taxes, make very sure you budget for those.

Like it or not you are going to need a spreadsheet of some kind both for your planned and your actual financial transactions.

Planning

How far ahead should you plan your budget? It's up to you but at a minimum 90 days ahead. Big businesses plan 1 year, often 5 or more years into the future. You are a small business just starting out and so that kind of planning, with all of the uncertainties before you is, quite honestly a waste of time.

By all means decide what you want your income to be next year, after 5 years. That's goal setting and it will motivate you. However, stay realistic otherwise you are setting yourself up to fail, and failure is the greatest demotivator, because we perceive it as a negative instead of as feedback on what didn't work that we can learn from.

So, for this step in the book we are going to provide you with some ideas on how to build a 90-day budget for your business from both an income and expenditure perspective.

One off outlays

Throughout this book we talk about the expenses your business is likely to incur. One-off outlays are common at the start of your business and might include at least the following:

- IT Equipment: Computer / Phone / Printer
- Insurance
- Business Registration fees
- Legal Guidance
- Financial Guidance
- Training and Development costs
- Marketing: Website build / Advertising / Printing
- Office furniture: Desk / Chair / sound and lighting equipment
- Production equipment
- Warehousing
- Delivery vehicles
- Materials for manufacture
- Patents
- Packaging

All of these costs need to be estimated (accurately), planned (what date will the expenditure be made) and recorded.

Continual out-goings

Once you have added the one-offs to your financial plan then consider the ongoing costs. These are the outgoings you expect to have to pay on a monthly or quarterly basis and may include:

- Subscriptions for memberships
- Software costs / subscriptions
- Stationary
- Monthly insurance payments – indemnity / car / phone / equipment etc.
- Monthly phone contract payments
- Premises and or utility costs
- Postage and packing costs
- Travel and delivery costs (car payments, mileage etc.)
- Regular payments to web developer etc.
- Bank charges
- Saving for taxes
- Loan repayments
- Wages for team / employees
- Materials
- Machinery maintenance

There are many things to consider so we suggest you go through the rest of the book before you develop your budget as we cover everything we can think of that you might need to plan for.

Monthly revenue

Ok, once you have planned your one-off and regular expenditure you need to plan your income to cover all of those payments plus whatever income you want to take out of the business.

Outgoings in month + your 'wage' = income needed

Right now, you are probably wondering if it's all worth it (it is!) and if you will ever make enough even to cover your expenditure (you will!). It is scary but imagine how much worse it will be if you don't budget and are constantly being surprised (not in a nice way) by what needs to be spent.

So how much do you need to make each month? More importantly, how are you going to make it?

How many product sales do you need to make? How many client sessions do you need to carry out?

How many people do you need on your fee-paying course?

The best way to calculate this is to work backwards from your target monthly income.

Let's assume your monthly outgoings (including one off payments in that month) are a total of £2,000. You want to take £3,000 out of the business as a 'wage' in that month. You need £5,000 of income in that month.

£2,000 out + £3,000 wage = £5,000

See the example on the next page, of how to work out what you need to do / sell in a month to achieve a net income of approximately £50k per annum. (***Fig 4.1 Budgeting).***

Financial goals – how do you measure success?

You yearly budget will help determine your financial goals. It's important to break those numbers into at least monthly records so you can always determine where you are against budget and make any immediate changes as needed.

Aside from financial goals it is important to look at other personal and professional measures for success. For example, growing your email list to 1000, 10 public speaking engagements per year, publishing 5 articles for national publications, buying a new car etc. Non-financial measures of success can often provide more personal satisfaction or sense of achievement.

See Fig 4.1 Budgeting on the next page as an example.

Love Being the Boss, Hate Business

Coaches (service provider) example:

Assuming I want to earn @ £50,000, only work 4 days a week and my expenses total @ £16,000 a year

Income generation table

	at standard fee	number required	Value	at discount fee	number required	Value	package 1	number required	Value	package 2	number required	Value
1 Personal 1 to one coaching	£100 per session	120	£12,000.00	£75 per session	24	£1,800.00	5 session for £400	10	£4,000.00	10 sessions for £750	10	£7,500.00
2 Speaking engagement	£500 per engagement	12	£6,000.00	£300 per engagement	12	£3,600.00	corp £1000 p/day	9	£9,000.00	corp contract £4000	3	£12,000.00
3 Book sales	£5 per unit profit	200	£1,000.00	£2 per unit profit	200	£400.00	n/a			n/a		
4 Online course sales	£1,000 per 3wk course	6	£6,000.00	£500 per 2 wk course	6	£3,000.00	n/a			n/a		
5 Other												
Totals			£25,000.00			£8,800.00			£13,000.00			£19,500.00

Grand total per annum before expenses etc.	Total per month average income before expenses etc.
£66,300.00	£5,525.00

			Hours required per week
Just 1 to 1 coaching	284 sessions which is 24 a month which is 6 a week	£25,300.00	6
Just Speaking	2 a month	£9,600.00	10
Corp Engagements	approx 2 days a month	£21,000.00	5
Book sales alone (4 books)	time to write and market a book 2 weeks / 80 hrs in total each book	£1,400.00	6
Online course sales	develop 2 per year and deliver 6 of each	£9,000.00	3
Other income	tbc		
		£66,300.00	30

Fig 4.1 Budgeting

Record keeping

You simply must make sure that you record every financial transaction in your business. A simple finance spreadsheet you can create yourself should contain both your income and outgoings and is enough for a small start-up. It might look a bit like this:

Your Company Name Here
Income and Expenditure
Business Start Date: xxx

Expenditure Record

Date	Reason for Expenditure	Payee	Amount	Payment Mode	Balance
		Totals	£0.00		

Client Fees

Date	Service provided	Client	Amount	Payment Mode	Balance
		Total Income to date	£0.00		

Remember also to keep all your receipts for the tax man! In fact, plan at least one day a month to work on your financial record keeping and admin.

CHECKLIST – DO THE MATH

Draw up your budget	☐
Work out how much you want to achieve _net_ in the first year	☐
Record _all_ of your income and outgoings	☐
Plan at least 90 days ahead	☐
Don't forget to budget for the taxman!	☐

So, you have what it takes,

and you know who you serve, why and how,

and you know there's a market for your business and what you want to look like,

and you have the necessary funds to get started and survive for a while,

What's next?

Love Being the Boss, Hate Business

My Notes and Observations

Love Being the Boss, Hate Business

My Notes and Observations

Love Being the Boss, Hate Business

STEP 5
PLAN FOR SUCCESS
(you gotta have a plan)

Why have a business plan?

Yes, you know what we are going to say next:

"By failing to prepare, you are preparing to fail."

Benjamin Franklin

And it is so true.

Planning the activity of your business is fundamental in ensuring its success. Why? We are so glad you asked, well here's a few reasons . . .

1. It gives your business a structure to work to
2. It enables you to measure your progress
3. It gives you deadlines to work to (which really will help you to get things done)
4. It helps you to avoid procrastination
5. It makes you accountable
6. It stops you forgetting to do stuff
7. It helps you to identify what works and what doesn't
8. It helps you to be organised and stay on track
9. It gives you motivational goals ad targets
10. It helps you to avoid overwhelm

That's just a few. There are many more. So how do you write a Business Plan for your Business.

How to write a business plan, format and presentation

Your Business Plan can be anything from a simple spreadsheet, listing activities and when they need to be done by, right through to a full on 'book' that records and analyses every aspect of your business. What will work for you is up to you however we would always advise you to keep it simple. For everything you do in business ask yourself this question:

Why am I doing this? If the answer does not include a tangible result that drives your business forward, then why waste time and effort (and maybe money) on it. Let me give you an example.

Example

Strategy 1.

I am going to spend an hour a day on social media, seeing what everyone else is doing and making comments and posting when the inspiration takes me. This way I will see what others are doing, learn from it and I will get known and seen, especially with my posts. I will also use paid advertising for my offers.

Time required per month: 28 – 31 hours

Interaction with ideal clients: possible

Consistency level: low

Costs £: High

Strategy 2.

I am going to spend a day each month developing content for social media that provides my ideal client with valuable information and shows them that I am the person to come to when they need help in that area. Some of that content will direct them to my website and/or offers where they can find solutions to their problems. I will schedule all of this content to upload automatically each day.

Time required per month: 8 hours

Interaction with ideal clients: likely

Consistency level: high

Costs: low

Which of these would you plan to do to drive your business forward?

Consider the audience

Is the business plan just for you? If not who else is it for? Employees, partners, investors? If it is just for you, keep it to a minimum – what needs to be done by when and what you need to do/get to achieve that. If it is for others, then consider what you need to add to a simple basic plan for that audience. For instance, if it is for partners / collaborators you will need to include the budget and how profits and costs will be split. You might also include a formal agreement between all parties as part of the document.

Write the business plan - not War & Peace

As we said before, keep it simple. A business plan should include as a minimum the following:

- Your budget (see previous chapter)
- Your list of activities, timed (at least 90 days ahead)
- Any resources / support you need to get things done
- All deadlines
- Collaborators details
- Your engagement strategy
- Your social media content plan
- Your time off

Easy to understand - main categories and bullet points and attachments

Executive summary

An overview of your business, it's values and its objectives for the coming year.

Contents summary

Literally a contents table

Business idea - types of coaching services/tools

More detail on your business and its operations. What you intend to do, how you will do it etc.

Target client (niche)

A detailed description of your ideal client and target market.

Market & competition

Details about your market such as where your ideal clients hang out (SM groups, online forums, physical places etc.). Your SWOT analysis and competitor research. Your marketing strategy for at least 90 days ahead

Marketing & distribution

The activities of your marketing strategy timed and dead-lined. The actual plan of how you will be seen in your market.

Sales process/landing the client/user onboarding experience

Your funnel, diagram or description of how it will work. A checklist for onboarding new clients. Detail on the client experience you are looking to provide.

Budget

Your full annual budget, taking into account everything covered in Step 4 with contingency planning built in. This needs to be reassessed regularly to avoid surprises and keep on track.

Additional resources - Partners/VA

Details of people and companies you work with, suppliers etc.

Timeline for execution

A fully timed, dead-lined action plan for your business. This must be assessed regularly and kept up to date.

How often it will be updated with actual results and adaptations

Plans for admin time and business assessment are essential. Get them into the full plan and detail them here.

Love Being the Boss, Hate Business

So, you have what it takes,

and you know who you serve, why and how.

and you know there's a market for your business and what you want to look like,

and you have the necessary funds to get started and survive for a while,

and you have a plan.

So, what's next?

My Notes and Observations

Love Being the Boss, Hate Business

My Notes and Observations

Love Being the Boss, Hate Business

STEP 6
BUSINESS OPERATION
(the icky admin stuff)

"Successful people do what unsuccessful people are not willing to do. Don't wish it were easier; wish you were better."

Jim Rohn

Now your business plan is complete, it is time to build the optimal framework and structure for your company. The eye-rolling, form filling, record keeping, frustrating administration work. Evil but necessary to start operations, find clients and build your business in a professional manner.

The following information is based on UK legislation (as of June 2021) and is provided as a guide only. It is recommended you take appropriate professional legal and financial advice, as required if you are based in other parts of the world.

Business structure

Let's start with how you need to register your business. The legal structure you choose will depend on how you plan to operate your business. The most popular structures for small businesses are to register either as a Sole Trader or a Limited Company.

A sole trader is the simplest option. As a sole trader, you as an individual own and run the company. As the sole owner you are entitled to the profits the company makes and liable for the business debt, if any, and payment of taxes. Registration as a Sole-Trader requires the completion and submission of several forms to the HMRC to register as self-employed.

https://www.gov.uk/set-up-self-employed

A limited company structure is where the business is a separate and distinct legal entity from its owner. Essentially, this means the financial perils and fortunes of the company are limited to the funds and assets held by the company. You can register your company online at the Companies House on Gov.UK.

https://www.gov.uk/government/organisations/companies-house

Other structures such as limited liability partnerships are available for consideration. Do your research to find out which is best for your business.

Deciding on the best structure for your business entirely depends on your specific needs as a business owner and your growth plans for the future of the business. Typically, small one-person businesses, tend to choose the sole trader route and those with plans to grow and build the business beyond one person, with the view of selling it as a going concern in the future, select the limited company route.

Irrespective of the structure selected, it is your responsibility as a business owner to be aware of your annual corporate, accounting and tax obligations at all times.

Finance, accounting and taxes

Once your company structure is decided and registered you can proceed and open a business bank account. There are many banking providers to choose from, it is recommended that you select one where you either have an existing relationship or they specialize in small start-up business accounts. Think about whether you want to do all your banking online or whether you need a local branch for face to face. And finally, are you trading in just your currency or accepting payments, paying invoices, in foreign currency. If you are you need a bank account that facilitates this at the best rates possible.

An important next step is understanding the basic accounting and tax record keeping and reporting requirements. At a minimum, daily income and expenditures records should be maintained and will be required for annual tax and corporate return filings.

Registration for VAT can be considered when the required threshold for annual sales is reached.

Within the first year it is advisable to hire an accountant to help you with the required annual financial filings and tax assessments. A good accountant who specialises in small business will also be able to help you draft annual budgets and provide gap analysis on variations from budget, as well as offering you a variety of relevant financial advice.

You may also wish to consider investing in small business accounting software, to maintain your books and records, depending on the volume and complexity of your business. There are plenty of user-friendly, low-cost options available to download. Maintaining accurate records is key from start of operations.

Protection

Securing the right level of protection for your business is key. If you need specific advice on the best structure of your business and its operations, then legal advice will be required. Legal support may also be required to draft client contract templates.

As your business grows you may require legal advice to register and protect the Intellectual Property ("IP") your businesses brand and products. Registered Trademarks protect the ownership of your businesses name, brand and logo from misuse by an unrelated third party. Registered patents protect the ownership and exclusive rights of use for specific products, inventions, processes that have been created by your business from being copied by unrelated third parties. Copyrighted work protects the use of your business written or creative work from being reproduced without your prior authorisation.

Over time, legal advice may also be needed if the business is expanded to include new partners or to manage the sale of the business or to represent and protect your rights in court.

The unexpected can and does happen. Professional Indemnity is a must have insurance for business which provides professional services to individuals or groups. Coverage can protect your business against claims for damages and legal costs that can arise due to any alleged act of negligence or breach of professional duty, in your day-to-day operations.

Public Liability insurance will be required if you work in others' premises, sell products or carry out works.

There are a variety of Insurance Carriers available in the market each with their own specific policy wording and coverage inclusions and exclusions. It is recommended that you choose a Carrier with a strong rating and reputation for working with businesses in your field. Most policies are structured to protect you from negligence claims, defamation and copywrite infringement. As your business expands additional insurances may be required to suit your business needs.

GDPR

General Data Protection Regulation (GDPR): The GDPR is a complex regulation that requires you to observe certain protocols in how you gather, use and manage personal data.

If you have any personal details about your clients including email addresses, bank details, date of birth etc., suppliers or other individuals in your business then these must be protected by law.

You have the obligation to protect data of employees and consumers to the degree where only the necessary data is extracted with minimum interference with data privacy from employees, consumers, or third parties.

If you register your company as limited you will be contacted by the Information Commissioners Office (ICO). You may need to pay a data protection fee to be included on their register. Unless you meet the exemption criteria you have to pay this so check carefully.

GDPR is complex and requires a book of its own, so our advice here is to read up on it and make sure that your business is compliant.

CHECKLIST - BUSINESS OPERATION

I understand how to set up and register my business	☐
I have planned my admin tasks and costs into my full business plan	☐
I keep clear and comprehensive records of all my business activity	☐
I have the insurances I need in place	☐
I understand the GDPR requirements for my business and have a strategy in place to control this	☐

So, you have what it takes,

and you know who you serve, why and how.

and you know there's a market for your business and what you want to look like,

and you have the necessary funds to get started and survive for a while,

and you have a plan,

and the icky admin is sorted, so what now?

My Notes and Observations

My Notes and Observations

Love Being the Boss, Hate Business

STEP 7
EQIPMENT AND SOFTWARE
(stuff you gotta get)

"It matters little how much equipment we use; it matters much that we be masters of all that we do use".

Sam Abel

When starting out, evaluating your tech needs can throw up a lot of mental blocks. Primarily because most business owners are not tech experts. We may not have all the information to fully assess our needs. In fact, we may not even know all the options that are available to us.

Lack of information drives procrastination. Procrastination comes from fear. Fear of making the wrong decision. Fear of making a mistake. We're now stuck, and we're frustrated, and no further along in the process to decipher our tech needs.

The escape from this tech nightmare is to keep it simple and take purposeful actions. The question is not 'what do I need?'. It is 'what do I need NOW?'. In order for the business to start operations, what do you need today?

Your big vision for your business may well to be as a service provider with millions of global clients or the next Richard Branson with multiple worldwide operations however, without some simple decisions to get started and get your message out there, you will probably remain invisible and unknown.

As a general rule, keep it simple, act in the present, plan for the future.

So, when starting out what do you really need? Well, that all really depends on what you want to do in your business.

How do you want to connect with your potential audience, and convert them to clients/customers?

Please note here that our advice is targeted at the small business owner providing a service or individual products and working from home.

The equipment

At a very minimum you will need a laptop, a fast, reliable internet connection and a printer. This alone will have you operational and able to start your journey to being visible online. It is personal preference thereafter if you want to add one, two or even three large monitors to your working configuration.

If you are considering quality video posts or going live on social media then a quality, professional camera and ring-lights are recommended. Similarly, if you are planning on recording audio courses or Podcasts, professional microphones are a must, or good quality on-ear headphones with a plug-in jack to your microphone. Pop Filters and booms may also be required depending on your audio equipment capabilities and the physical set-up and configuration.

A wide variety of this professional grade, quality equipment is available for purchase at relatively low cost. However, we highly recommend you pause before purchasing. Unless you plan to use this equipment from day one, then it is better to wait and buy as needed. The technology for this type of equipment is upgraded regularly, with many new versions and additional features being added. It is more likely that you will buy it cheaper or with more functionality when you know what it is you are buying and how you intend to use it.

The software

The urge here is to subscribe, buy or download a wide variety of software solely based on their promise to transform or automate how you work. In order to use these tools and technology confidently and competently, most software/online technology tends to have a steep learning curve to master first. If you find the software to complex, then you won't use it, no matter what delights it promises.

Stay focused on the primary goal, get started and find clients, and build on the tools you need as your business grows.

Again, a simple assessment of your immediate business needs can help a lot. The key to success is to make the client user experience as easy and straightforward as possible for them to work with you.

The essential tools to get started are:

- Business subscription to an online video and audio recording system e.g., Zoom, Google Meet etc.
- Online scheduling or booking system like Calendly, Google etc.
- Customer Relationship Management ("CRM") system like Mailchimp, Zoho
- Contract and document delivery system like jotform, docusign
- Payment processing system like PayPal, WorldPay, Stripe etc.
- Automated social media management like Hootsuite, Buffer etc.
- Content creation platform like Canva, Visme etc.
- Cloud Storage like OneDrive, DropBox etc.

There are plenty more options available for your current and more advanced needs, including software to bundle your technology selection, but theses basics should get you started.

A wide variety of specific software to support your business including communication tools, blog or newsletter design and editing, or video and audio recording, editing and tagging is also available. As well as, podcast external hosting accounts, design software and URL links to promote your visibility and connection with prospective clients.

Avoid the overwhelm. Depending on your needs there is tech to help you solve it. Start simple, make a plan, grow purposefully. It does not have to be stressful, just concentrate on what you really need and ask for support and advice if you are stuck.

It is also good idea to regularly audit of your software and subscriptions and update those you are using and unsubscribe from the ones you are not. Consider, do you actually use it? Does one tool do multiple tasks? Are they cheaper to access as a bundle? Do the various systems interact well? Are there any others that could help streamline your work processes?

There is always going to be new and exciting tech available. The key is to figure out what you need to help you run your business efficiently and allow your clients to connect with you in the most efficient manner.

Other considerations

Wherever you work from, ergonomics is an important consideration:

- Is your office set up to suit you?
- Proper lightening?
- Airflow?
- Is your desk at the correct height so you are not working in an uncomfortable hunched over manner?
- Is your desk adjustable so you can stand when taking calls, working or recording video or audio?
- Is your chair comfortable?
- Does it have sufficient Lumbar support?
- Is it adjustable?

As your own boss it is important to consider all of these and customise a comfortable environment for you to run your business. And if you have others working for you, their health and safety is a must, so you need to ensure you are compliant with all the workplace health and safety regulations.

The variety of tools and technology available to support your business operations expands rapidly, adding functionality to help streamline your operations and connectivity. Plan to grow and expand your knowledge and tech suite as your grow your business but always purchase based on need, rather than desire.

Love Being the Boss, Hate Business

So, you have what it takes,

and you know who you serve, why and how.

and you know there's a market for your business and what you want to look like,

and you have the necessary funds to get started and survive for a while,

and you have a plan,

and the icky admin is sorted,

and you have all the equipment you need.

Now what?

My Notes and Observations

My Notes and Observations

Love Being the Boss, Hate Business

STEP 8
THE BUSINESS OF BUSINESS

(clients and stuff)

"No matter how many customers you have, each is an individual. The day you start thinking of them as this amorphous 'collection' and stop thinking of them as people is the day you start going out of business."

Dharmesh Shah, Co-Founder of HubSpot

Call to action

However you market your business, through networking, paid advertising, generic growth by posting and commenting on social media, whichever way you do it you will need a call to action.

Something that gently nudges your prospective clients towards you, to visit your website, to read about your courses, to book a discovery call with you for your service or visit your shop to buy your products.

The key thing is to market in a way that makes people want to contact you, look you up and get to know you, and what you do, better.

And when they do, make sure that wherever possible you capture their email address. If they want to register for your course, email address, join your Facebook group, email address, download your free pdf from your website, email address, call you on the phone, email address, buy something, email address.

Why? Because that's how you grow your email list and that's how you grow your marketing.

With an email list you can send out regular content, newsletters, notices about events, discounts and special offers directly to people who have already been interested enough to give you their email address. People who are already interested in what you do, warm leads.

Vetting process & why it is important

There are people out there who will get in touch with you, join your groups, attend your networking events etc. simply to grow their business by connecting with your connections and or by selling to you.

You know the ones, when you accept a friend request and immediately there is a direct message asking if you are interested in finding out more about their X, Y and Z. These people will generally not buy from you so don't waste your time on them. By all means leave them on your mailing list. They may never buy from you, but you never know!

What you are looking for is people who are genuinely interested in you and what you have to offer. Vet out the time wasters and concentrate your efforts on these people instead. That is where your business is.

Onboarding process

You are at the point where you have a nicely warmed up prospect who has shown a real interest in you and your business and now wants to discuss working with you or buying your stuff.

This is a yippee moment, celebrate it.

It is also the most crucial time in your relationship as business owner and customer and as such there are some things to think about here.

1. *Listen very carefully* to what they are telling you they want to achieve. Your job is to help them find ways to solve their problems and achieve their goals, with your service or product. Are you sure you can do that?

If not, if you cannot be sure that you are the right service or product for them, then don't take them on as a client. Instead, help them by recommending them on to someone you know and trust who is better placed to help them, or a different product more suited to their needs. (As a business owner you need to build a network of peers for just this moment, as well as all the support and fun you will get from the community).

2. You have established that you can help them, you are the right business for their needs. Now is the time to manage expectations and give your new client confidence about what working with you means.

a) Set up a schedule for your services or product delivery

b) Establish the overall goal and initial priorities of your client

c) Explain how the relationship will work

d) Make sure they are happy with the arrangement and if they have any questions

e) confirm your fee / price

Engagement Contract

If you are selling individual products to individual customers you are unlikely to need a contract unless that product is high priced and may require ongoing service.

If you are providing a service then it is good business sense to create an agreement with that client detailing the services you will provide, at what cost, how and when and including your joint obligations to each other.

Any service contract should include as a minimum:

1. Definitions

Client Details: Clients' name, address and email address and phone number.

Fees: How much and on what payment plan basis.

Session Criteria: how often and for how long each session and until when.

Schedule: agreed and booked when / how often.

2. Fee Structure and Program An overview of the fees payable by when and what for.

3. Signatory section for the client and the service provider

4. Terms and conditions such as

- Your commitments
- The clients' commitments
- Your expectations
- Your agenda for each session
- Ethics and confidentiality
- Cancelling and rescheduling protocols
- Contract termination protocols
- General terms

By way of an example see ***Fig 8.1*** below, a simple coaching contract.

Our Coaching Agreement   *Company name or Logo here*

This agreement is provided for information and forms the basis of our coaching relationship.

1: Definitions

Name:_____*(Client's name)* **Coaches Name:**_____ *(Your name)*

Clients Address:
_____
_____

Clients Email: _____ **Clients Phone:** _____

Fees: £_____ per month based on a _____ month coaching schedule

Sessions: ____ per month for ____ months as mutually agreed and booked

This Agreement is between: _____ (Client) and _____ (Coach)

2. Fee Structure and Program

This agreement commences on _____ for an initial period of _____ months and is thereafter subject to mutually agreed extension.

1. ____ sessions per week / month of _____ hours duration

2. Sessions will be in person / via zoom / by phone (*delete as appropriate*)

3. Sessions will take place on the dates and times agreed at the first session

4. Payment will be made in advance of each session via bank transfer / cheque / PayPal / other (delete as appropriate) as agreed.

I have read this document and confirm that I understand the terms of this agreement:

Signed by:

Love Being the Boss, Hate Business

Client Name: _____ Date: _____

Signature: _____

Coach Name: _____ Date: _____

Signature: _____

3. Terms and Conditions

The Companies commitments:	1.	The company will provide coaching to the client as agreed.
	2.	The Coach will provide a professional and confidential service in order to support the client in achieving their goals.
	3.	Contact between sessions is permissible by email
Client commitments:	1.	You will pay the fees as agreed in this document
	2.	You will attend each session as arranged
	3.	You will be honest and open in your sessions in order to get the best result.
Coaching expectations:	1.	You are responsible for the results you get from this coaching; no guarantees of success are made in that regard.
	2.	This is not a medical service, and you understand that this is not a substitute for counselling or therapy services.
Agendas for each session:	1.	The agenda for each session will be agreed mutually in advance of the session.
	2.	The agenda will be based on your needs and can be changed by you at any time.
Confidentiality / Ethics:	1.	All sessions will be carried out in a professional and ethical manner with your wellbeing a priority.
	2.	All session notes, discussions and recordings are confidential and will not be shared unless required by law.
	3.	You contact information may be used by the company from time to time to advise you of information that may be of interest to you.
	4.	Your details will not be sold to or shared with 3rd party organisations under any circumstances.
Cancelling and rescheduling protocols	1.	Sessions cancelled less than 24 hours prior to the arranged date and time will remain fully payable.
	2.	In any other circumstances your session payment may be refunded, or the session rearranged.
Contract termination protocols	1.	The Company or Client may terminate this agreement at any time by giving 7 days written notice of intent to terminate.
	2.	All fees due must be paid before the contract is terminated

General terms	1.	The Company will not be held liable for any distress, physical or mental, or any arising medical condition which you believe to be a result of your coaching.
	2.	Should you feel distressed or unwell at any point you must advise the coach immediately.

Additional Information:

You will approach each session in a serious manner in order to fully benefit.
If you are unwell or distressed, please let your coach know immediately so the session can be halted.
Coaching can be uncomfortable and evoke upsetting emotions. Be prepared for this.
Your Coach will be considering your mental wellbeing as a whole throughout this process.

Fig 8.1: Example Coaching Agreement

For one-to-many service provision

We are talking about courses, programs, workshops, group sessions, webinars etc. here. Where you are delivering to more than one person at a time.

The principles here are the same as for one-to-one service provision in that your audience has a problem/s to solve and you are going to help them to find a way to solve it with your service.

They will have responded to your call to action to book into your event. They are warmed up and ready to learn from you. That gives you a responsibility to ensure that what you give them is what they expect, what they need.

Online events / courses / workshops – more than just delivering

As a writers coach Ali runs a course called **Everything You Need To Know To Develop Your On-Line Course** (check here for details and the next available session: https://alibagleycoach.samcart.com/products/everything-you-need-to-know-about-online-course-development-

For this book we list the basic principles you need to consider which are:

- What is the subject / topic of your course?
- Who is your target attendee?

- What is their problem / pain point?
- 1 to 1 or one to many?
- What do you have that will help them solve their problem?
- What is the purpose of your event/program/course?
- What media will you use?
- How will people book and pay?
- Timings, what suits your attendees?
- Are you doing this alone or in collaboration with others?
- If so, who is responsible for what?
- How will you structure your event/program/course?
- How will people get to know about it?
- Do you have the right equipment?
- Live or pre-recorded?
- Free or paid?
- Will you develop Giveaways?
- Will you include networking?
- What is your marketing plan?

As you can see there is a lot to consider even before you begin to develop your service event.

Plan programs 3 months in advance

Effective marketing of your service should begin about three months before the event. In this way you can target your ideal attendee with teasers and value in advance. They will get to know you and understand what you are about. You will focus on their problems and how to solve them. When you then launch your offer, at least two weeks before the event date, they will be ready and waiting to join up.

You don't have to actually have the completed event ready three months beforehand, just know the outline and design your communications based on that and the principles listed above.

Slide decks for webinars and courses

This is a book on its own however, when you are producing your content for your courses, webinars and workshops a PowerPoint (or similar) slide deck is the ideal way to deliver that content. People learn in three key ways: seeing, hearing and reading. A slide deck enables you to provide content for all three learning styles.

You can include graphics, pictures, charts and video (with or without sound). A slide deck is also a great aide memoir for you as well as being the focal point for your attendees.

A few things to remember:

1. Is it clear and legible?
2. Does it relate to your narrative?
3. Is there a mix of words / graphics / videos / images?
4. Does it look professional?
5. Keep it simple, don't fill a slide with everything you are going to say, just show the bullet points, or a simple image.

    Remember, less is more.

So, you have what it takes,

and you know who you serve, why and how.

and you know there's a market for your business and what you want to look like,

and you have the necessary funds to get started and survive for a while,

and you have a plan,

and the icky admin is sorted,

and you have all the equipment you need,

and you know exactly what you are offering, how to market it and how you are going to deliver it.

So, what's next?

My Notes and Observations

My Notes and Observations

My Notes and Observations

# Love Being the Boss, Hate Business

STEP 9
WEBSITE

(where the interaction happens)

"If you can offer a free tier that provides a lot of value, it will naturally help your product to spread much more rapidly."

Melanie Perkins, Co-founder of Canva

WITH OUR GUEST GILL FOUNTAIN OF 38 PARTNERSHIP

To have? Or have not?

Why would you want to have a website for your business?

PRO's	CON's
Clients expect it	It costs money
You can be easily found	It requires upkeep
You can control what people see	It takes planning
You can have a shop in it	It takes time
People can book calls with you	It will only work if you continue to sign post people to it
People can contact you easily	um . . .
People can get to know you	um . . .
Easy to write and share blogs	
Easy to share a link to it when networking	

Yes, it's takes time and effort however, the Pro's far outweigh the Con's and that is why we have a website for our businesses, it's our credibility calling card.

Build yourself? Pay?

How tech savvy are you? How much time do you have? What do you want to achieve from your website? All questions you need to ask yourself.

Love Being the Boss, Hate Business

Yes, there are plenty of places online where you can design your own website, and if you are looking for a simple site to tell the world who you are, what you do and how they can come and work with you or buy from you, then maybe that's the way for you to go.

We both tried the 'do it yourself' approach. The results? Zero traffic, zero leads, zero sales. You see we didn't understand the power of things like back links, SEO and key words, we still don't to be fair, so although we were sharing the links to our sites during networking and in our social media, nothing was really happening.

And that is why, for this chapter, we are handing over to Gill who really does know about this stuff . . . take it away Gill.

Who is Gill Fountain?

Gill, Tell the world about who you are and what you do

Thank you, Susan and Ali; I am delighted to receive your invitation to be a guest author in Love Being the Boss, Hate Business.

Hello, let me start by giving you a little background about myself.

I started my business decades ago; at the time, I never thought I would make it through the first three years, let alone 30. My children were tiny, and I, unexpectedly a single parent, struggled with a foundling business in the toy trade.

My highs were a strong realisation that I had managed to keep my children fed and watered as they reached their teens - and every time, my business jumped another level.

I worked with the top toy buyers in the UK, exhibited at all the main exhibition halls. Imported and exported and helped to design the next generation's toys. I took new designs from production to high street level marketing traditionally and, with what moved into the new digital marketing and designing websites.

As buying patterns changed, we altered our business to 38 Partnership, Branding and Marketing, helping business owners to increase the visibility of their business without it costing a fortune.

I moved towards teaching business owners, followed by invitations to write and speak at national and international events.

How to purchase a domain

Can you outline here what a domain is, why it's necessary and how to get one.

Your domain name (also known as URL - Uniform Resource Locator) is how people find your website. i.e., www.bestukcoach.co.uk

> **TIP**
>
> Always research the name you want to use; the most basic way is to search in google using just the words. Often a favourite domain or business name will be used by large companies or a famous person. If you continue to use the same name with perhaps a .net or .biz where you would have had .co.uk or .com you will either be consistently promoting someone else or fighting to get onto the first few pages of the search engines.
>
> To buy a domain name go to the likes of 123-reg or GoDaddy, add your preferred domain and click to see if it is available. They often discount the first year when buying two.

> **TIP**
>
> Be aware that they will try and upsell; choose wisely; you don't require lots of domain names.

Business email

Having a business specific email is a must in order to separate your personal and business email traffic and to appear professional to your potential and current clients.

You are going to share your email address everywhere so if for instance you are looking for executive clients and your email is bubba@cheekychops.com then that might not instill the greatest confidence in your potential clients. If, however your email address was Victoria@executivecoachsolutions.com they might be more inclined to contact you!

If you are working with a website developer, they will show you how to buy and set up your business email. Alternatively, you can go online and find out how to do it there.

I would add that people tend not to take Hotmail email addresses seriously; inversely, having a Gmail address as an extra does come in handy at times, especially when claiming your Google My Business account.

Purpose of website

The key purpose of a website for your business is to get you seen and known and liked and trusted so that people will want to buy your services or products from you.

It is the place where you have complete control over what your clients get to know about you, so it should reflect your personality.

It is basically your shop front. Here people can look through the window and see what you have on offer.

You can outline your services including your packages and prices and how to book. You can have a contact form to make it easy for clients to get in touch with you, you can communicate with your ideal clients through your blog page, and you can start to build relationships with your site visitors so that they get to know, like and trust you.

Design/layout/format

Your Landing Page: The first thing your site visitor sees, has to encourage them to learn more and click on through your site. It's all about bounce.

Bounce Rate:

Calculated by the number of times visitors arrive on your website and leave without moving to another page.

Let's dive a little deeper. Your website bounce rate - your aim is to get it as low as possible; although typically, anything under 50% is good, some of our sites are as low as 5%. A lot of how to achieve this is by planning how your potential clients will use the site - carefully planning every path leading from page to page. This is where an experienced website designer will gain you business.

Here is Ali's:

> I am here, in the space between your now and your desires for the future, ready to lift you up to all you can be . . .

For Coaches, For Authors, For Small Business Owners.
A wealth of Support, Services, Community, and Interaction awaits you in these pages

Where do you want visitors to go next? To your menu, to see what else is there? So, onto your Home Page then. Here they will find the menu of all the content in your website and can choose where to visit next. This is a great page to put your free pdf. Something that gives value to your ideal client that they can download for free in exchange for their email address (kerching – email list). Your web designer will also set up links to your social media from this page.

Here is Ali's Navigation/Menu Page:

HOME
ABOUT ALI
BOOKS
STORY ROOM
CONTACT ALI
SERVICES
BLOG

COMFORT CORNER
with Ali

The Top Ten Things That Get in the Way of Writing a Book

GET MY FREE PDF BOOK

So next your visitors might want to learn more about you and so they will go to your 'about me' page. Here you can tell them your story, everyone loves a story, about you personally (if appropriate), you as a business owner, why you do what you do, what your hopes and goals are, what you are up to next and so on. It's your story so you decide.

The key here is to engage and resonate with people, help them to see you as someone they would like to work with and know more about.

You might also put your certificates on this page and testimonials, or maybe a button to direct them to your testimonials (if they are on another page).

If you have written books or have other products to sell you could create a page to talk about those and include links to make it easy for people to go and buy them.

Another page might include your videos. Video blogs (Vlogs), bitesize teaching videos, videos about your courses and programs, any kind of video content. People like videos.

You might want a page specifically for your services and packages, explaining what you offer and making it easy for your visitors to buy or make enquiries.

A contact you page is a must have, with a form to complete with their details and what they want to know/discuss with you.

And of course, a blog page. Where you write your blogs and that is set up so that you can get a link for each individual blog to share on your social media.

It is in the planning, look at each page, where are you leading your visitors? Can they find their way back, is the menu easy to find, do the headings make sense and relate to the content? Most notably, are you leading your next potential client into a brick wall, is there a call to action, or does it lack clarity?

Are they still asking themselves, I am not sure what service they are offering, what do I do next?

People like to have clear instructions. All these factors are very easy to overlook. Carefully planning or choosing an experienced web designer who is invested in you and your business, AND fully understands how to design your website so that the search engines will rank you, will pay dividends in the growth of your business.

Number of content pages

Depends on your budget and your business requirements. The content outlined above is a basic minimum for any business site. Your web developer will advise you on the best set up for your business.

User functionality / Interaction - capture email, download freebies etc.

Designing a website that is easy to use takes a lot of planning. There are many 'pretty' websites that receive no traffic and never lead to engaging a client or making a sale.

Here are some questions to answer:

- Is it pleasing to look at, shall I stay?
- Can I read the content clearly, are there natural breaks?
- Do the headings relate to the content? Am I confused?
- Do the colours clash, is the font too small, is it all the same?
- Can I easily find out what I will get out of it? What are the benefits?
- Do I like this person?

That's about 10 seconds into your website, and we are not even on the second page.

People like to follow instructions, they enjoy a clear path, they don't want to waste time looking, they get frustrated and move onto possibly one of your competitors - who may not be as good as you - but have an easier to use website.

> **TIP**
>
> Having a downloadable free pdf helps to grow that know, like and trust relationship that has to happen, especially when engaging a coach. It helps your potential client as they are getting something where they can gain value. It also helps you as now you have their email with the option to not only send them to the link to get their free pdf, but you have received their authorisation to send other relevant information. You are growing your database!

Add an image of the front cover, pop in a sign-up box and click you've started warming up your potential next client. Of course, it's not so easy as that; there is a real science behind colours, fonts, call to action's and even, would you believe, buttons, however at this point, focus on giving away something of value to gather their interest.

Photos / Stock images

A word of caution. You can't use any picture you find on the internet for your website. Unless you are using your own images then there may be licensing fees to pay. Be very careful with this because misuse of licensed images could cost you a fortune.

Back-end hosting / Admin & analytics

To publish a website, you have to have:

- A domain name (URL) - TIP: Insist that you are in control of your login details

   And

- A web hosting platform. This is the physical space where the code for your website lives and runs.

Until these are in place, your website will not appear - even if your website has been designed with Search Engine Optimisation (SEO) built into it before publication.

When building and maintaining your website, you will have the option to work inside the back end, where you can add and amend your website's content. Depending on the template or platform you use will depend on how much you are allowed to amend.

Many sites also have their analytics (not to be confused with Google Analytics). These will give you a less in-depth but convenient overview of how your site is performing.

> **TIP**
>
> It is essential you keep hold of your login details.

SEO / Google analytics

Let's start this section with a word of warning. Many, and I mean many web designers, sell SEO as an add-on. If it hasn't been thought through, or there is no understanding of how SEO can be built into a site in the designing process, it can be enormously costly.

To achieve Search Engine Optimisation (SEO) is not one, but hundreds of decisions to be made beforehand, with the planning of the site, during, how the website is laid out, how the layers work together to enable the bots to index the site and enable searches, after publication with accurate page titles and descriptions.

SEO is a vast topic, and it changes so often that most of the template platforms bought off the shelf cannot keep up. This is why a website is not found, or it will slowly slip down to page 6 or 12 or have no organic reach.

Visibility is key to a business owner; communicating is vital. You can have a far better service or product than your competition; however, if they are better at marketing their business or have engaged experts to help them, they will be easily found in the search engines. There are many more ways to increase visibility; however, having a fully optimised site saves a lot of costly time and money.

> **TIP**
>
> One area on how it is scored or ranked is how fresh your site is. Regularly add or change content to your site, small changes make a difference.

> **TIP**
>
> Enable Google Analytics - working on the basis that if GA is not enabled, how can google find you?

Once your Google Analytics is set up you may choose to ignore the fantastic stats that are found when delving through layers of information. However, venturing inside, you will find this and a lot more:

- How many visitors you are getting?
- Where they land and what pages they visit
- How long they are staying on each page
- You can identify what pages are failing
- What your bounce rate is and how to correct it
- Where people arrive from, even what social media platform!
- Are they local, national or international?
- What search engine they have used

There is even a map showing how they have moved through the site.

Understanding how to use this information will help you know what is working and, if not, how to either correct it or address your marketing to increase sales is an excellent free tool to have at your fingertips.

e-Commerce / Shop

What do you have to sell? Are you selling your books in hard copy, so you need to get buyers info to package and post? Are you selling pdf's that you want to just send out automatically on purchase? Whatever you have to sell it needs to be simple for the customer to buy otherwise you will lose them before they get to the checkout.

Professional advice on setting up your e-commerce is recommended to avoid costly mistakes.

Getting paid

You've designed your website, adding your products and services but how you want to be paid.

How you do this is how much you want to automate the payment side of your business. In the higher ticket services, we have found that clients do not like to process large amounts via a website. They want to speak to a person, possibly set up a payment plan, receive an invoice and pay via bank transfer or credit card.

They are happy to utilise a secure payment process for the lower ticket services or membership sites. It may be as simple as linking to your business PayPal account (not personal). Set up a PayPal account for business - we have found the non-paid for one works perfectly well.

There are many other payment platforms; they must be secure and take your client to a separate payment encrypted interface to complete the transaction. Stripe is brilliant with membership site payments nationally and internationally and provides excellent data and backup services.

> **TIP**
>
> Bank and payment charges can rack up and diminish your bottom line. The costs vary enormously, and a word of caution, it is always best to research and compare prices; there are many offers where the initial period looks far cheaper only to have a higher % added at a later date.

The points I have added above are really the very tip of an iceberg, however they are extremely important as a means of saving time and money and I hope you have found them valuable.

If you have any questions, please contact Gill Fountain at gill@38partnership.co.uk and she will be more than happy to answer them for you.

Love Being the Boss, Hate Business

ATTENTION Business owners

What are you doing to increase your Visibility?

Talk to Gill Fountain

www.38partnership.co.uk/how-to

38 PARTNERSHIP

Brand • Marketing • Visibility

Love Being the Boss, Hate Business

So, you have what it takes,

and you know who you serve, why and how.

and you know there's a market for your business and what you want to look like,

and you have the necessary funds to get started and survive for a while,

and you have a plan,

and the icky admin is sorted,

and you have all the equipment you need,

and you know exactly what you are offering, how to market it and how you are going to deliver it,

and you know what to do to have a fully interactive google analytic enabled website.

Now what?

My Notes and Observations

My Notes and Observations

STEP 10
MARKETING AND DISTRIBUTION

(get out there)

"Sometimes, it doesn't hurt to ask. I have been in the news many times just by calling on the news channel and asking them about featuring my business."

Lori Cheek, Founder of Cheekd

This area is probably the greatest challenge and headache to new business owners. Most of you just want to help clients or make sales. Starting out we are trained as skilled and specialist in our chosen fields, not marketing, sales and social media experts.

Accept that while sales may be a very dirty word to you, you are going to have to sell if you want to have clients and grow your business. Stop fighting it and avoiding it and figure out the best way to do that for you. This means finding an ethical way to communicate your brand and offer to your niche clients.

Mastering the foreign skills of marketing and sales may seem daunting, but they can be done elegantly by being authentic and staying on brand. Marketing, sales and building community is 100% about communicating and using your brand to sell your services in an authentic, relatable and purposeful manner.

Leverage and position your brand

If you cannot clearly and simply articulate what you do, then no-one will understand it. Be clear on your Unique Selling Points ("USP's") and use this to communicate your area of expertise. Note that USPs are actually pretty rare so if you don't have one, don't worry, just make sure that what you do have is as good as it can be and get that message out there.

When you were establishing your brand, you will have identified the key topics or messages that define who you are as a business owner and what you do. Leverage this brand platform to position you in the market.

Stay on brand. Be consistent. Be radically relevant – be prepared to pivot and position your core brand content and concepts to relate to what's impacting your potential clients today. Staying up to date with what is happening in your market community and the world and being able to proactively demonstrate how you can help will allow you to become a leader in your field.

Route to market

Decide your route to market and what channels and systems you intend to use to connect with and attract your potential clients. There are several online platform options such as Facebook, Instagram, Twitter, LinkedIn, Clubhouse, YouTube, Pinterest and many more…… You may also consider blogs, newsletters, guest posts, hosting or guest appearance on podcasts, speaking and networking events, media interviews or even writing a book.

Not all platforms will suit you or your brand. The key is to pick two or three platforms that are most applicable and master those first. You can grow from there. Taking on more than that at the start of your business will be overwhelming and distracting. Many of the platforms have several tools and functions too. A good idea is to set a quarterly review to identify what is working and what can be added or removed.

Content matters

Just randomly posting on social media is not a plan and will only cause uncertainty and confusion about your brand and your offer. Your content and messaging should be intentional not accidental. Start with the core pillars of your brand. Consider what you are offering and communicate how it will help others. Marketing and promotion should only be about how you can help your clients. A strong plan should have 4- 6 weeks of content prepared.

Content should always be about what problem you are solving and should be designed to inspire, connect, engage, impact and convert potential clients to actual clients.

1. Inspire = The attention grabber. Your potential clients stop

scrolling to read and like your post

2. Connect = Potential client starts to follow you to learn more about what you offer
3. Engage = Potential clients responds to your call to action and opens dialogue
4. Impact = You respond, listen to their problem and give something of value that will help their situation
5. Convert = potential client likes how you helped and wants to work with you. You get paid.

This five-step process will guide your potential, exact match, niche client on their journey to work with you. If you miss a step in the process, then you miss the opportunity to work with a new client.

Content shared on social media should have a clear call to action. Always ask for a response or comment. A good way to identify and measure content that works is to look at your competitors posts. Ignore the number of likes they have and instead look at the number of comments they received. See who responded and why?

Ask yourself, why did a post work, what did you like about it, how did it make you feel, did it motivate you, did it seem like it was written just for you?

Blogs and newsletters allow you to have a captive audience to expand on your messaging. They work differently to social media as the reader has already subscribed to the content. They want to receive and hear what you are sharing.

If someone signs up for your material, then they are clearly telling you they find your content useful and trust you. Use blogs and newsletters to solve your client's problems. Don't worry about giving away all your good material. You could give a hundred people the same ingredients to make a meal and get a hundred different meals in return. By sharing willingly, you will build trust and convert clients.

Blogs and newspapers are a great source for social media content. Using excerpts, you can create content for several posts and use social media to drive traffic to your website.

Always work smarter not harder with your content. Create your brand content for one platform and then repurpose it across all your other platforms. This helps drive consistency in messaging and are an excellent way to build rapport with your audience.

Attracting and building your community

Building a strong, valuable community is strategic. You want to be able to connect with potential niche clients who actually want what you are offering. Simply following random people on social media who you think might be in your target niche, is like trying to find a needle in a haystack.

Trying to sell people services and products they don't want or need or is waste of your time and will leave you feeling exhausted and disheartened. To sell with integrity you need to believe in and demonstrate that what you are offering can help and make a difference in your clients lives.

Blogs and newsletters are a great way to build community and more importantly build your own client database. Social media is a great way to attract others into your community to communicate and share your offer however, it is not helpful for collecting potential client contact details. Often accounts get frozen in error, platform algorithms change or go out of vogue. This can greatly impact your connection and accessibility to your community. Always try to get potential clients to connect with you on email or through your website so you can capture their details for future marketing, events and promotions

Consider joining existing groups and associations that mirror your niche clients' interests and actively participate in the conversations. Add value. Be disruptive with your perspective. This will generate curiosity and interest in you and attract your niche clients to your platform.

Re-marketing is a great way to gain visibility and attract attention. If you've seen an engaging post, watched an inspiring Ted Talk or read a thought-provoking book, share it. But always, always add your comments. Why are you sharing it? What did it mean to you? How does it connect with you and your brand? How will it help your clients?

Promoting and supporting others builds credibility and trust.

Again, don't worry about losing followers. If they move on, then they were not your niche clients. Instead, consider all of the benefits and recognition you will gain by aligning yourself with other respected experts in your field.

Finally, when building your community, remember the law of large numbers does not always apply. Look for sanity metrics not vanity metrics, i.e., it's better to have a small audience that engage with you than a million followers (unless you want to sell a book!). You have selected and developed your niche with purpose. Misaligned clients can cause disruption. It is far more substantial to have a lower number of followers that are engaged and connecting with you than a higher number of random disassociated followers. People buy from people they know, like and trust.

Referrals and testimonials

By far the most effective way to build your business in an authentic and ethical way is through referrals and testimonials. They do the selling for you. What other people have to say about you and your business is a huge asset for you. Collect them as much as you can, after every workshop or training session, after your satisfied client no longer needs you, from colleagues and friends.

As a minimum you need these on your website, in your sales copy, in your books, on your courses and they are essential in your advertising.

The best way to get them? Ask, simple as that.

And for goodness sakes, get your testimonials, contact info and bios added to absolutely everywhere, your FB / Insta / LinkedIn / Twitter / membership sites / everywhere!!

Love Being the Boss, Hate Business

Here are a few of ours:

Thanks again for last night Ali, it was really nice attending your second lesson on writing skills, and your approach is really inspiring. Looking back to my story from the beginning and seeing all the troubles and challenges I was passing through, it really boosts my self-confidence and makes me more sure about the next goals for my family, my business and my career.

Thanks again for your teaching and for your passion.

Michele, Italy

Susan has helped me realize my potential and goals! She really helped me focus and believe in myself which has resulted in my business growing and expanding way beyond what I ever thought was possible. Thank you.

Craig, England

Ali's calm, patient style of coaching is enough to destress anyone who needs some inner calm. Her clarity and focus leave you knowing you can rely on her to get to the root of your issue and to help you through it.

I would highly recommend Ali as a coach and am looking forward to my next session with her.

Aisha, Germany

I have had the pleasure of working with Susan several times recently and have always found her to be attentive, creative, curious and wise. She is always a pleasure to work with.

Jo, London

Ali, great session tonight, loved it and learned so much, thank you.

Marcia, England

I met Susan by chance, as often happens in networking and we realized pretty quickly that we had complementary skills that could come together in an amazing way.

Since we have been working together my admiration for this lady and her abilities has grown and grown. Not only is she fiercely intelligent, but she also has real heart. Everything she does is driven by who she can help and how. I recommend her without hesitation to anyone looking for a way forward in their professional development. She has opened my eyes to so much, she will do it for you too.

Alison, England

Susan is a remarkable listener, with broad understanding and a great vibe and energy. She has a lot of experience. She knows when and what to ask, in order to help figure out your focus and priorities. She has valuable life experience, which I found so relevant for a global view of different life situations like mine. I am very grateful for her help to reset my perspective and expectations so positively and simply. She really managed to help me. She is kind and nice and genuinely good person and an amazing coach and woman.

Andreea, Dubai

Susan is so easy and fun to work with. Her approachable manner made it easy for me to share and her positive coaching motivated me to make the changes I needed to. . . Highly recommend working with Susan.

Michaela, England

Thank you, Thank you, Thank you Susan. I'm so much happier in all areas of my life after working with you. I'm a new woman with a new outlook and I'm loving it. Did I say, thank you?

Christina, USA

> *Ali has a unique gift for being able to take your thoughts and help you translate it to a mission on paper like no other.*
>
> *Her ability to help me hold the mirror up and dig deep is some of the best time I've invested.*
>
> *Working with her I can truly say she delivers the outcomes she promises.*
>
> **Carlyle, England**

> *Thanks again for inviting me to the session yesterday afternoon. It was very powerful and inspiring.*
>
> *I particularly liked the way you two involved the audience in a passive, non-aggressive way without putting anybody on the spot.*
>
> *I'd love to see how this journey continues.*
>
> **Bernd, France**

One more thought ....

As uncomfortable and strange sales may feel to you, the skills needed to be successful are not that different to your core business skills.

- Connect and build rapport.
- Ask open and leading questions about what your potential client is looking for from you.
- Listen to their responses.
- Using a conversational approach to sales is genuine, authentic and builds trust. It also quickly allows you to identify if the potential clients fall within your niche or not. It's much better to say no to the wrong client, than to work with them.

Love Being the Boss, Hate Business

So, you have what it takes,

and you know who you serve, why and how.

and you know there's a market for your business and what you want to look like,

and you have the necessary funds to get started and survive for a while,

and you have a plan,

and the icky admin is sorted,

and you have all the equipment you need,

and you know exactly what you are offering, how to market it and how you are going to deliver it,

and you have a fully interactive google analytic enabled website,

and you marketing strategy and plans are in place and you are still standing.

What's next?

My Notes and Observations

My Notes and Observations

Love Being the Boss, Hate Business

STEP ELEVEN
LAUNCH YOUR BUSINESS

"Your work is going to fill a large part of your life, and the only way to be truly satisfied is to do what you believe is great work. And the only way to do great work is to love what you do."

Steve Jobs, Founder of Apple, Inc.

GET OUT THERE

DO YOUR THING

BE SUCCESSFUL

So, your business is up and running based on a solid foundation with everything in place.

Is that it?

Love Being the Boss, Hate Business

NEXT STEPS
PLANNING FOR GROWTH
(Onwards & Upwards)

"Ignore the hype of the startups that you see in the press. Mostly, it's a pack of lies. Half of these startups will be dead in a year. So, focus on building your business so you can be the one left standing."

Jules Pieri, Co-founder and CEO of The Grommet

Reality check

Once your business is set up and running it will require continual maintenance and improvement. Your business is an ongoing commitment.

Continuous training and CPD

Never stop learning. Put some money into your budget for ongoing training. Add new skills, develop new methodologies, gain more experience and knowledge and keep making connections.

Regularly assess risks and opportunities

Things change, all the time. What might have been a threat last year might become an opportunity this. Regularly review your risk register and update it.

Creating multiple online revenue streams

As you grow and develop as a business owner consider trying new things. Maybe write a book, develop online courses, get involved in collaborations. There are so many different things you can do, not just to make money but also to become known and respected in your field.

Is there a better way to do things, keep watching and learning from others and see how the world changes?

Learn from those who have already made the mistakes and those who have succeeded (often the same people). Read, follow the news in your industry or specialist area. Who would have thought in 2019 that by 2021 just about everything would have gone online? Stay informed and up to date.

Continually reassessing your strategy

Like we said, things change, the world changes, people change, we change. You have your plan, reassess it regularly and update it as you and the world change.

Don't go too big too fast, master each stage

This is maybe one of the greatest risks to your business. It's like a beast in a cage and if you let it loose too soon, before you are able to control it, it might just turn around and bite you.

At each stage of your journey make sure you have mastered your business. From your initial training, then in setting the foundation for your business and then in each new area you grow into. Step by step, stone by stone.

Have a big vision - what/where do you want to grow to?

If you take yourself back to the beginning of your journey to become a business owner, you had a dream, a vision of what could be for you and your business. The decision to become the Boss was just the start of that journey. It is important to remember and hold onto that vision and keep moving towards it every day.

It is harder in the beginning as your vision can be clouded by the start-up administration, learning technology platforms and marketing strategies. It is easy to start feeling overwhelmed and defeated as all your time and energy is being consumed to just get you out of the starter gates.

This will change. Stay the course. Early on it will be helpful to write down your vision or find a picture or object that represents your vision and keep that in your workspace as a reminder on those difficult days to keep going.

Break your vision down into actionable goals and determine the process you need to execute on those goals. Remember every action your take puts you a step closer to delivering on your vision. Use your vision as inspiration and yardstick. It shows you how far you have come and where it will take you.

Don't lose sight of your vision or lose your passion. Keep reconnecting with your reasons for starting the journey and you will make it!

How will you grow? & When?

"There is only one way to eat an elephant: a bite at a time."
Origin unknown

In other words, pick ONE concept, or area of focus at a time. Immerse yourself in the actions necessary to complete that task. Remind yourself that you are on a learning and a growth curve. Once you have implemented and mastered your task, move on to the next. That's how you grow and expand your capabilities and services.

If you start to feel overwhelmed, then slow down. Re-assess what you are doing and why. Review you action list and timeline for reasonability. If you need help, then look among your peers and the coaching community to find someone who has already achieved what you are doing and connect with them for advice. Think baby steps and remember the elephant metaphor, just take one bite at a time.

Another way to grow is to collaborate. Just because you are a solopreneur you do not always have to do everything alone. You can partner with other business owners to learn, practice, create and deliver. Join forces for a purpose while each of you maintain your own businesses. Variety in what you do, and offer will broaden your audience much quicker and help you grow steadily.

Collaboration also adds a certain authority to your venture, people will see you as someone others want to work with and there has to be a reason for that right?

Recruit team / Outsource

The easy but unhelpful answer is hire when you can afford to.

Within every business there are always the elements of the work we enjoy doing and the work we do not enjoy doing. At the outset you will likely have to do it all yourself in order to get visible, get clients and grow. At this stage banking your income and monitoring your expenses, so that you can start to create reasonable profit from Day 1, is the priority.

When you are established and have the budget to get help look to hire a skillset that provides strength where your skills are weak. Determine the tasks that only you can do and those that can be outsourced to a support role. It's also important to make sure your new hire is the right fit so that you can work well together.

Determine what skills you are looking for and estimate how many hours a week it would take a capable professional to get the job done.

There are thousands of Virtual Assistants and outsourced experts out there, the key is to know exactly what you are looking for and what your budget is.

If you want to grow, then you will eventually need help. A one-man-band style approach will keep you small. As soon as you can hire help, do it. You can use platforms such as fivver, your own website or social media platforms like LinkedIn or other outsourcing websites, to find the help you need at a price that works for you. Where possible, check out recommended sources first.

Financial goals - how do you measure success?

Success comes in many forms. Yes, money is important, you have to pay the bills of course. Money is not the only way to measure success. Growing your following, making new connections, getting great referrals and testimonials, having booked out courses and programs.

When you set your budget maybe include some less tangible targets and check regularly to see if you are on track to reach those as well as your financial goals.

Measuring the effectiveness of your marketing

This is about identifying what works. Which posts get the most engagement, which ad for your course brought in the most sign ups, which products are selling the fastest!

Keep an eye on this because you might otherwise be at risk of wasting time and money on what does not work.

Manage your time - coaching/admin/time off

And last but not least, your mental health and wellbeing. No matter how much you love what you do it can still tire you out, overwhelm you, stop you from eating properly, prevent you from taking exercise and it will be hard sometimes.

Make sure you recharge when you need to. Actually book time out in your diary for family, friends, relaxing, exercising. And keep that time sacrosanct. Remember you are your brand, your product and your business so if you go down, the lot goes down. There's no sick pay for the self-employed.

So, your business is up and running based on a solid foundation with everything in place,

just a few final words . . .

Love Being the Boss, Hate Business

FINAL WORDS
TIPS FOR SUCCESS AND BUILDING RESULTS
(now you're cooking . . .)

"All our dreams can come true if we have the courage to pursue them."

Walt Disney, Founder of The Walt Disney Company

1. Perceptual positioning - keep checking in / check your reality & expectations

Keep on top of everything in your business. Check that you are on track with your budget. Assess what works and what doesn't. Update your risks regularly. Restate your targets if you have been overambitious, it's not failing, it's just rejigging.

2. Review your overall plan quarterly

Your plan is the backbone of your business, so you need to keep it up to date because things change really quickly. If you know what's changing and make adjustments early on, then you can avoid big nasty surprises later on.

3. Weekly Priority Execution Plan

Plan weekly. It's a simple little thing. Take half an hour to plan your week before the week starts and you will be better placed to stay on track, not miss anything and probably find a little free time as well.

4. Weekly marketing plan

Think about what marketing you are going to be doing specifically on a week-by week-basis. So, develop and schedule your social media posts at least weekly.

Think about how soon before up-coming events you need to start promoting. Plan it out as part of your weekly execution plan (above).

5. Market research never stops - what more can you do?

Keep reading, keep listening, keep watching. Liaise with colleagues and discuss trends. Ask your potential and existing clients what they need right now, it might be different from yesterday. Use polls, posts asking questions and surveys.

6. What's going on in the industry?

As above, keep reading, keep listening, keep watching.

7. The importance of continual education (CDP)

Learning and growth is a lifelong journey for all of us. Invest in yourself to improve your knowledge and skills whenever you can.

8. Connected community - build network to share ideas/practice sessions

The other coaches that you connect with are going to be one of the biggest assets of your business. Share knowledge with them, learn from them. Maybe start working in collaboration on books, courses and events.

Practice your craft on willing subjects. Network with them and for them, recommend them to others, that is authentic, ethical and will enhance your reputation.

9. Get a coach for each stage of where you are going

When you need support to continue to grow as a person and a coach/business owner a personal coach can be gold dust. If you try to do everything on your own, battle through the overwhelm, manage all the admin and paperwork, do all your own marketing, coach, deliver courses, write books, sell products, well you will probably explode. Get help when you need it. It's the only shortcut to success we know.

10. Identify obstacles - are they unique/personal to you? Are they real? Are they physical obstacles?

We define an obstacle as a thing, person or situation which prevents you from moving forward. Think, is this an obstacle of my own making (limiting belief, lack of confidence) or is this something external. Identify this first and then determining a strategy to overcome it will be easier.

Where necessary, particularly with internal obstacles, make sure to talk them out with a third party, friend, coach, colleague. Ali is a Geographer of Emotions and uses emotional mapping in her coaching and courses to elicit emotions in order to examine them and better manage them so that you can move forward from a position of strength and surety.

To find out more about emotional mapping see the back of this book.

11. Always connect & build from the heart - be authentic and passionate

Honesty, integrity, passion. Just three of our core values in business (and life). We hope that you will always bring these to your business. To be honest your business reputation might depend on them.

12. Niche down - be strategic not pushy - don't come off as desperate or devalue your offer

You will have worked out your niche (Step 2). You will have absorbed the advice about marketing and branding (Steps 3 and 10). You offer value, you are there to help your clients solve their problems.

If you were a dentist you would charge for the treatments you give, if you were a retailer, you would charge the price on the packet. What you do is priced at its value.

Do not compromise your value.

13. Be a planner - plan every week/program/social media/time off in advance

We cannot stress this enough. Make a plan, review the plan, action the plan, update the plan. It is an essential tool for the success of your business.

14. Set a budget for each new program launch

We haven't talked specifically about pricing, it's a massive subject and depends on your service, your audience, your offer, your skills, and so on and so on. What we have talked about is budgeting (Step 4).

So, as well as budgeting by year and by month, whenever you start a new project in your business, such as a program launch or course development, create a separate budget for this that sits within your overall budget. It will help you to make a better analysis of profit and will keep things tidy and easier to manage.

15. Read - everything and always

Continue your professional development always. Read, learn, progress, develop new skills, master those you already have.

16. Build your references and testimonials

Set up a file or folder to save all of your references and testimonials and feedback. This will be one of your greatest assets. Every time you advertise or publicise your business you need to include a testimonial to give it weight and show you as the go to person for your service.

17. Plan content for 3 months at a time - repurpose old content

We have talked about planning content (Step 10). Build a portfolio of posts and blogs and images. Re-use and recycle these.

Remember only a few people will see your content the first time you post it, so using it again means it will still be new for some people and will remind the others. Plus, repurposing and reusing content is going to save you hours of work.

18. Always be open to adapting

Things will change all the time, you will change. Your business will change. You must be able to continually review and reassess your business and adapt to changes in order to continually thrive.

19. Have fun, be in the moment, love what you do

Our last tip.

You are at work a lot. You will have ups and downs, success and challenges. Enjoy the ride, every day is an adventure.

What's next?

Well, you tell us, you got this . . .

We would love to hear how this book has helped you, about your business and what you do to make it a success.
Email us at:

ali@alibagleycoaching.co.uk   or   susan@inmyownlane.co.uk

EXTRA NOTES PAGES FOR WHEN YOU NEED THEM

My Notes and Observations

My Notes and Observations

Love Being the Boss, Hate Business

My Notes and Observations

Love Being the Boss, Hate Business

My Notes and Observations

Love Being the Boss, Hate Business

My Notes and Observations

Love Being the Boss, Hate Business

My Notes and Observations

My Notes and Observations

My Notes and Observations

My Notes and Observations

Love Being the Boss, Hate Business

My Notes and Observations

My Notes and Observations

My Notes and Observations

My Notes and Observations

My Notes and Observations

My Notes and Observations

My Notes and Observations

Love Being the Boss, Hate Business

My Notes and Observations

Love Being the Boss, Hate Business

My Notes and Observations

Love Being the Boss, Hate Business

My Notes and Observations

ABOUT THE AUTHORS

Ali Bagley

Wife. Mother. Grandmother. Dog lover. Friend. Traveler. Lateral Thinker. Pillion Rider. Zip Wire Enthusiast. Rotten Cook. Technophobe. Clubhouse newbie. Skinny Latte addict. Pizza junkie. Leo. Team Player. Grey, not Blonde. Collaborator. Funster. Liverpool Supporter. Constantly on a diet. Loves a Challenge. Lives to support. Identifies as a citizen of the World.

Ali is a Business Impact Coach, Writers Coach and a qualified Project and Proposals Manager. She is an author of guides for coaches starting out in their business and various journals and other business support books. She is also a Geographer of Emotions, helping people to grow and develop personally and professionally through the methodology of Emotional Mapping.

Her background is corporate project and proposals management, leading teams winning multi-million-pound contracts in infrastructure. She went to university at 41 years old and graduated with a BA (Hons) in Business and Finance Management in 2009. She has successfully run independent businesses for many years, before and after her time in corporate, gaining great insight and understanding of the pressures that being a small business owner can bring.

Throughout her career Ali has coached and written, these are her two passions. From running Weight Watchers meetings in the 1990's to running her own businesses in Insurance and Retail, her life has been a rollercoaster of highs and lows, both personally and professionally. Ali totally embraces all of the learning experiences that have brought her to where she is today.

She believes that to be able to help others achieve, you need to have learned from failure, to know joy you must first experience pain. She has been knocked down more times than she can count but has always got up again.

Ali is now living her best life, full of confidence, self-belief, love and purpose. Her journey now is to bring that light and positivity into the lives of others, through her coaching and her story telling. Ali is also very proud and excited to be the Director of Business for Emotional Mapping UK Ltd and Bertagni Consulting srl.

Susan Lane

Mother. Daughter. Sister. Friend. Dog lover. Adventurer. Global Traveler. Author. Avid reader. Personal development junkie. Curious. Podcast addict. Public speaker. Clubhouse moderator. Guest blogger. Country music fan. Foodie. Creative cook. Frothy cappuccino drinker. Fiercely independent. International. Leo. Leader. Goal-setter. Goal-getter!

Susan is an International Impact Coach, Risk Consultant and NLP Practitioner specializing in inspiring and supporting Entrepreneurs, Executives, High-performing and High-achieving Individuals to advance their passion for the possible and elevate their influence and impact.

Her coaching practice, In My Own Lane, help her clients progress their careers, personal lives and mindset to build lives they desire and deserve. By combining their passion and purpose, gaining absolute clarity on their goals, learning how to manage risk and make decisions, and overcome their limiting beliefs, Susan helps her clients design their personal roadmap to results.

Susan delivers personalised and targeted programs to help her clients upgrade their personal and professional behaviors and refine their strategies and practices to achieve their goals, accelerate their performance and create sustainable long-term impact.

She believes that while you cannot always control what happens, you can always control how you react. Her coaching helps her client's step into their personal power so they can live their life by design, not default.

Susan is an influential, results orientated leader with over 15 years global experience in corporate strategy and risk management. She has spent her life living, working and travelling overseas and brings an excellent global perspective to life and work situations. Following many years in the Board Room, leading global teams and speaking at international industry events, Susan decided to use her career learnings and experiences as the foundation for her coaching practices and methodologies. Aligning her leadership and risk management skills with her desire to connect with and help people and her love of writing, reading and psychology has transformed her personal and professional life from full to fulfilled.

Having finally put down some roots Susan is now based in the glorious Surrey countryside. She is mom to her daughter and two Yorkshire terriers and is working on completing her Business Psychology degree and writing her next book which discusses the four pillars of her coaching practice: Fear, Passion, Risk, and Action.

RECOMMENDED READING AND MATERIALS FOR YOUR BUSINESS

Books and stuff

The Magical World of EMME - Eliciting, Mapping and Managing Emotions by Ali Bagley & Marco Bertagni

Planning to Inspire – the essential handbook and planner for coaches to get their business activity organised by Ali Bagley & Victoria Morley

The Coaches Resource Directory – techniques, models and processes for new coaches by Ali Bagley

The River of Life – a journey into emotional geography by Marco Bertagni

Fearless – the workbook for the journey into emotional geography by Marco Bertagni

Countermove – a guide to the art of negotiation by Ralph Watson

Own Your Purpose & Realize Your Potential – experts recount their adventures to success by Leslie Thomas Flowers with contribution from Gillian Fountain

My Accountability Journal – The coach's tool for between session accountability for their clients by Ian George and Ali Bagley

Hygge Journal and Organised FIND YOUR PLACE - A Nordic Inspired Journal for Balance and Calm by Victoria Morley

Love Coaching, Hate Business – the number one best selling business support book for coaches by Susan Lane and Ali Bagley.

Courses

How to Build a Practical and Resilient Foundation for Your Business – https://alibagleycoach.samcart.com/products/how-to-build-a-practical-and-resilient-business-foundation-

How to Get the Writing Skills You Need to Grow Your Business – https://alibagleycoach.samcart.com/products/how-to-develop-your-writing-skills-to-grow-your-business

Everything You Need to Know About Online Course Development - https://alibagleycoach.samcart.com/products/everything-you-need-to-know-about-online-course-development-recorded

BUSINESSES THE AUTHORS RECOMMEND

38Partnership

In Your Own Lane

Ali Bagley Coaching

Emotional Geography UK LTD

Love Being the Boss, Hate Business

ATTENTION Business owners

What are you doing to increase your Visibility?

Talk to Gill Fountain

www.38partnership.co.uk/how-to

38 PARTNERSHIP

Brand • Marketing • Visibility

Love Being the Boss, Hate Business

in My Own Lane...

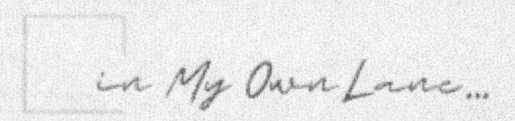

...means taking responsibility and control for your choices and the quality of the life you live. Being brave enough to define your own success and happiness and live your life, your way. By facing your fears, pursuing your passion, re-evaluating how you view risk, and taking purposeful action you create and live your life by design, not default.

Are you looking to level up? Ready for results? Want more influence and impact?
Do you know that you are made for more? Something more than you are today.

Whether you are planning your next big goal or project, pursuing a promotion, changing career, relocating, starting a business, growing a business, launching a side hustle, learning a new skill, reassessing your relationships or considering making a major life decision, if you are looking to transform your future and make your dreams your reality, then Impact Coaching will empower you to envision and create the life and lifestyle you desire and deserve.

Specializing in inspiring and supporting Entrepreneurs, Executives, High-performing and High-achieving Individuals to advance their passion for the possible and elevate their influence and impact, Susan is an influential, results orientated leader, risk specialist, international coach and NLP practitioner who delivers personalised and targeted programs to help her clients upgrade their personal and professional behaviours and refine their strategies and practices to achieve their goals, accelerate their performance and create sustainable long-term impact.

If you are ready to achieve you ambition and create your roadmap to results, contact Susan at susan@inmyownlane.co.uk

Ali Bagley Coaching

You are a coach, building your business is your priority, yet you are not a business person by nature or trained.

You want to write a calling card book as a marketing tool, you want to create an effective online course, and you want to increase engagement with written content on social media. But you need help.

Ali will guide you, support you, advise you and share her knowledge and experience with you as a published author, certified business impact coach and APM qualified project manager.

Everything you need to know about her services, books and courses and all her contact details can be found at:

https://linktr.ee/alibagscoach

Emotional Geography UK Ltd. The home of EMME in the UK

Eliciting, Mapping & Managing Emotions

The International Coaching Platform that brings the methodology of Emotional Mapping for personal growth and professional development to individuals, corporations, organisations and educational institutions.

Course, Counselling, Journeys and Games, all based in emotional geography, brought to you by our Geographers of Emotions. Over 40 skilled, experienced and talented individuals from all over the world.

To find out more about what we do, how you can take part and even join the delivery team, please contact Ali at:

ali@emotional-geography.com

Love Being the Boss, Hate Business

Printed in Great Britain
by Amazon